Zen Time ColorScapes

RICK CHEADLE

Creative Worx Publications

Adult Coloring Books
By: Zen Time ColorScapes

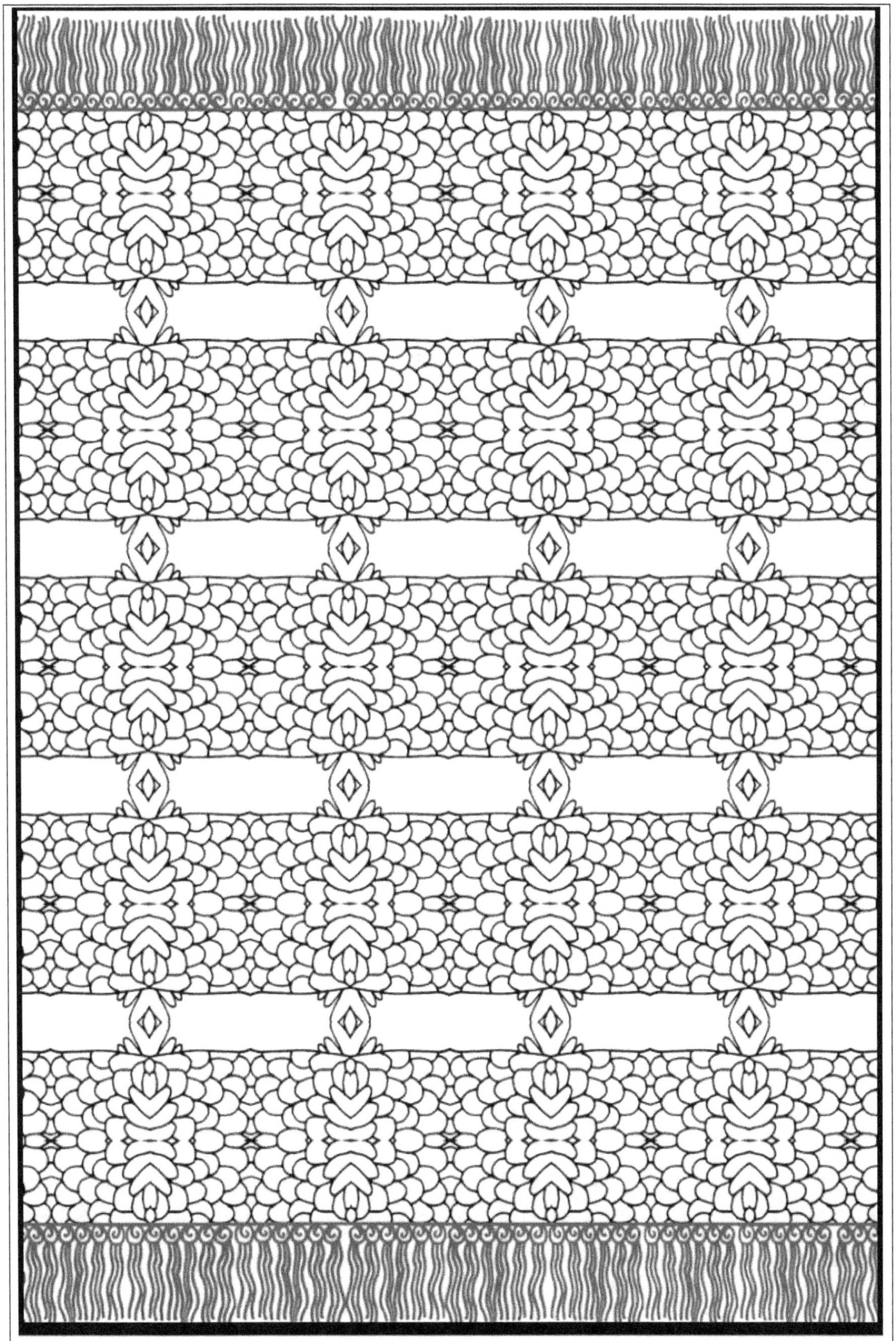

be.you.tiful

www.ingramcontent.com/pod-product-compliance
Lightning Source LLC
Chambersburg PA
CBHW081240280526
45787CB00006B/2741
* 9 7 8 1 5 1 9 4 8 7 7 5 9 *